REACHING FOR THE SKIES

Sumitra Bhattacharya

REACHING FOR THE SKIES
Sumitra Bhattacharya

Published by Qurate Books Pvt. Ltd.

© Sumitra Bhattacharya

Published in 2023

Disclaimer: The author would like to acknowledge that some of the photos have been sourced from the Internet sites and she has no copyright on these. Any error is regretted

Creative inputs by Alpana Chowdhury
Design inputs by Sohini Bhattacharya
Compiled by Nilanjan Bhattacharya

ISBN: 978-93-5898-256-5

Qurate Books Pvt. Ltd.
Goa 403523, India
www.quratebooks.com
Tel: 1800-210-6527, Email: info@quratebooks.com

Author's Note

I would like to thank my niece Alpana Chowdhury, my son Nilanjan, and my daughter-in-law Sohini for making this book happen.

I have penned down my life's journey with the hope that it may serve as an inspiration to those young girls who are trying to break the shackles of a conservative environment while tackling personal hardships.

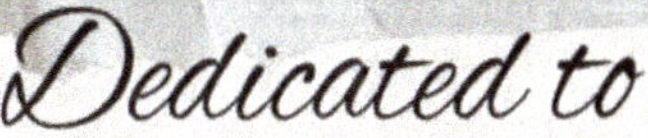

Our revered Gurumaharajji, Shri Shri Mohanananda Brahmachari, without whom my family and I would have been totally lost in this world. He, through his blessings and divine protection has constantly guided us throughout our life. I place this book at his lotus feet and continue to seek his blessings for all of us.

Introduction

The idea for this book emerged one lazy afternoon, when a niece and I were chatting about bygone days. Her curiosity about my career as an air-hostess in the 1950s took me down memory lane to an exhilarating period of my life. Those were early days of commercial air travel in our newly independent country and I was indeed lucky to be a part of it. While the aircraft we flew in were small ones like the 21-seater Dakota or the British manufactured 44-seater Viscount, some sans air-conditioning, the passengers were generally larger-than-life. The challenges we faced were very different from what the cabin crew faces today.

Our pilots often faced life-threatening situations that required them to be ace navigators, flying through difficult terrain and unpredictable weather conditions. We worked as a team, ensuring comfort and safety of our passengers whatever the circumstances. It was an exciting job and I enjoyed every moment of it, challenges and all.

As the afternoon wore on, and the setting sun filtered in through the window into our room, I narrated several stories to my niece who sat engrossed in my narration. "You have to record these events," she suggested.

My son walked in just then and immediately warmed up to her suggestion. "Let's write a book" he said.

And so, this book happened. My daughter-in-law joined in as the designer of the book. I thank all of them for their enthusiastic participation in giving shape to my memories.

While more than half a century has gone by since I picked up the gauntlet to carve an independent life, and much has changed since then, a lot still remains the same. Even today, girls have to fight for their independence and encounter numerous obstacles along the way. The choices before them are many. My generation had very few options. But asserting themselves and making a choice of their liking can still be a thorny path for today's women, especially in non-metro towns. To them I would like to say, don't give up your dreams.

Happy dreaming! Keep reaching for the skies!

Daring to Dream

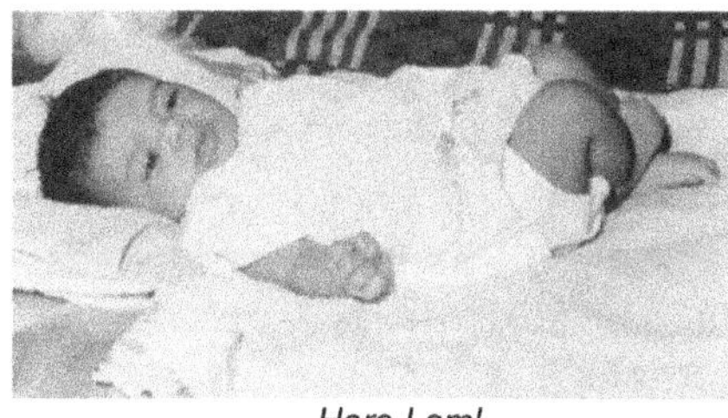

Here I am!

Our country was a little less than a decade away from achieving its historic Independence from British rule, when I arrived in the Sinha household, on March 25, 1938, a bonny baby all of seven and a half pounds. The youngest child, I had three brothers and two sisters who doted on me.

With my eldest sister

My brother with our family car

My father, Rai Sahib H. P. Sinha, like many educated Bengali men of the time, was in 'government service', as they would say. He was the Deputy Accountant General with the Government of India during British times, now known as the office of the CAG. We had a very comfortable life, residing in a sprawling bungalow built on a land parcel close to an acre, in the posh Hailey Road locality of Delhi. Our home "Radha Niwas" (named after my mother) had eleven bedrooms, one out-house of four bedrooms and a row of staff quarters to accommodate four families of our domestic helps, two big garages which housed our Chevrolet car, a luxury in those days.

The house had five large gardens which had peacocks, two dozen ducks, dogs, a parrot enclosure and two cows from whom we got fresh milk every morning. Apart from this house, which was our primary residence, we also had a four-bedroom independent single-storied house on Babar Road which was put out on rent.

Agrasen ki Baoli

Our house was near Agrasen ki Baoli, a step well of significant historical importance and now a heritage site, which featured in the Hindi film PK and recently, in Sultan, among others. In my childhood it was overgrown with vegetation and was considered as a haunted place in the various adventurous games we played there!

As was the norm those days, my father was a father figure to numerous cousins, even distant ones, who stayed with us over extended periods of time either on work or for their academic pursuits. Given the seniority of my father, we were privileged to have a close circle of friends which included some very prominent personalities like Sarat Chandra Bose, Shyama Prasad Mookherjee, famous writers like Prabhat Mohan Bandyopadhyay and astro-physicist Meghnad Saha. Some of them would stay with us whenever they were in Delhi. Our out-house, which was done up really well, would often be offered as a courtesy to nawabs and royal families of princely states when they visited Delhi and we would play host to their entourage and guests. In all, a very well-off and lively household!

My father

In 1942, my father took up a senior role with the royal family of Jaipur, and he was allotted a palatial residence in the Pink City. While the rest of the family continued to live in Delhi we would often shuttle between the cities over weekends and holidays. So, I grew up in the lap of luxury, at least initially.

However, tragedy struck in 1944, when my father suddenly fell ill and passed away soon after. I was only six then when life took a drastic U-turn. With nobody to guide my

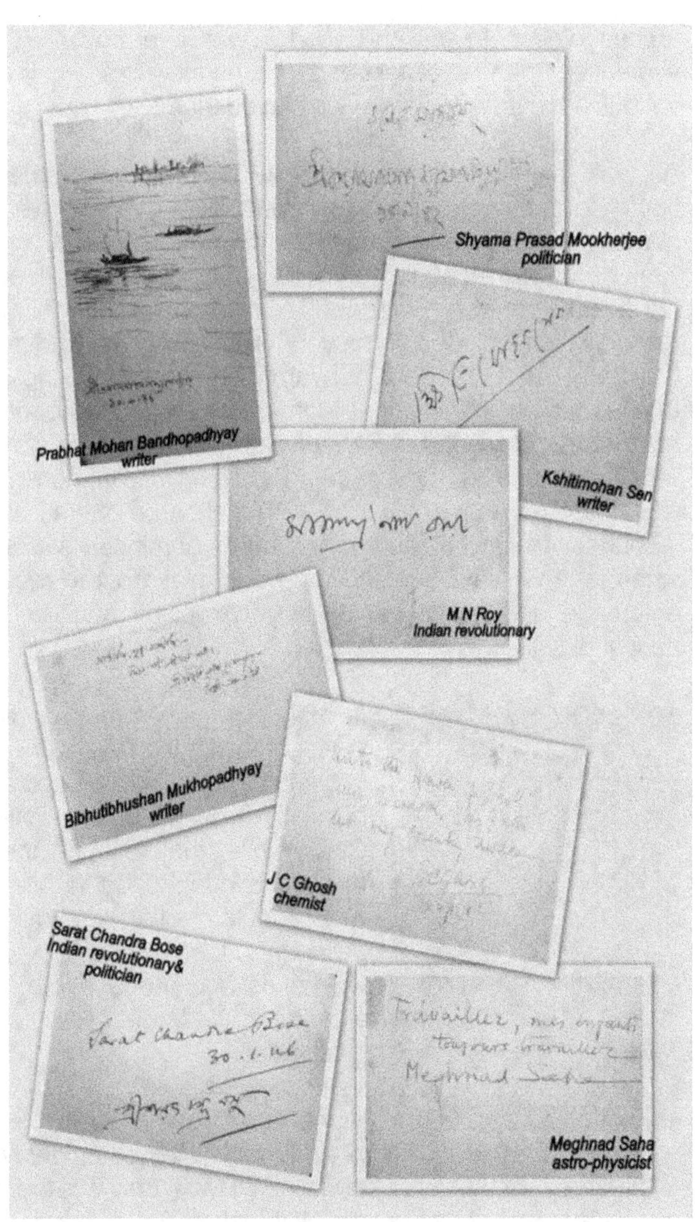

My treasure trove

[4]

My mother

mother in money matters, our family saw its financial position going downhill quite rapidly. Our family used to keep much of our money and jewellery in a private bank. To our immense bad luck, the bank collapsed in 1946. By the time my brother, who was a co-signatory of the account with my mother, arrived from Calcutta where he was working, it was too late. The bank had closed shop and we could not withdraw anything. We lost most of our deposits and valuable family jewellery kept in their lockers!

Soon the days got tougher and we had to find ways to generate some running income. Since our property was quite large, we decided to rent out one half of the house and that is where our ordeal began. Initially our tenant was at his best behaviour and very prompt with payments but then as his business flourished, he started making unsolicited offers to buy out the entire property, which we obviously refused. Now as a process we would collect the rent from him every month and sign a receipt, which he would prepare. Never did we imagine, that all this while he had hatched a devious plot to take over our property. On one such occasion, he made the receipt and then left a small space above the signature box. We did not suspect a malafide intent and signed the receipt as is. The tenant later filled up the space stating that an amount of ₹ 17 thousand had been paid as an advance to buy the house from us for ₹ 2 lacs. Not only did we not want to sell our house but now we were fraudulently made a seller at a fraction of the market value! This was the most shocking development for us because besides the fact that my father had expired recently, my eldest sister was also grappling with serious medical issues. We filed a legal case against the tenant for fraud and then started our agony of seven long years of multiple court cases and hearing dates. This took a severe toll on the family, both, emotionally and financially.

While we were fighting multiple court cases, the country too was going through turbulent times. Riots broke out in 1946. There were rumours that Connaught place and Hailey Road would see violence. A cousin of mine insisted that we move house since it was unsafe to stay there. He had his own independent bungalow at Lodhi Road provided by the Government of India and we all shifted there with our dogs, ducks, and birds in tow. During our stay with our cousin I saw much of bloodshed and looting all around. The men of our family and friends had to patrol the streets at night while the women folk slept on the higher floors fervently hoping those would be safe enough. Corpses on the road, and outbursts of blood-curdling sloganeering gave us shivers but we braved it all, and tried to live normal lives going to school or work when there was relative calm, and even conducting marriages.

While we were away, just so that the tenant would not illegally occupy the rest of the house, we let out the remaining part of the house to another family hoping that this would protect the property to some extent possible. However, as we realised later, this too turned out to be a folly. Both the families got together to try and take over the property. Though the first tenant got imprisoned for forgery a couple of times, he would manage to be out on bail every time and the case continued. During this time our house on Babar Road also had to be sold to fund all these expenses. Eventually the prolonged cases took a toll on us and finally we gave up.

In 1952 we looked for ways to sell the property and eventually found a coal trader who was willing to buy but as you can imagine we had to do the sale at a distressed price. So what could have been sold at a significant cost was sold at just ₹2 lakhs in those days. And how did the coal trader manage to vacate the house? Well, he hired four or five goons and put them up in the outhouse, got the local cops on his side and then had the thugs harassing the women folk. With no option left, they just left the house. Thus, ended the saga of Hailey Road at this point in time. Through these difficult years we shifted home often and finally settled down in Karol Bagh.

As a young child, from the age of six I witnessed tremendous upheavals and turbulence-- passing away of my father and eldest sister, loss of property, financial troubles, riots and destruction. All this left an indelible impression on me which probably shaped my approach to life.

And then, that momentous day arrived, August 15, 1947, when we gained our Independence from foreign rule! I was in class five, in Lady Irwin School, on Canning Road, when all of us, to

Lady Irwin School

our pleasant surprise, were given sweets and chocolates and a copper plate commemorating Independence Day.

As part of the celebrations, students from our school were to perform a group dance at the Red Fort, in front of Pandit Jawaharlal Nehru. For some reason, though I was a good dancer, I was not part of this group. Disappointed, I went to the school principal and requested her to include me in the dance. However, it was too late then for her to accommodate me. But seeing my enthusiasm and pluck, she chose me to garland Panditji. What a thrilling moment that was for me! Only nine years old, and I garlanded the first prime minister of India.

Dreams in my eyes

When I was around 14 years old, I went with my mother and sisters to Shimla, for my sister's recuperation after an illness. We put up at a modest hotel which was opposite the luxurious and iconic Cecil Hotel on Mall Road. One night, as we were strolling in the compound of our hotel, I looked at the twinkling lights of Cecil, and dreamily pronounced, "One day, I will stay in that hotel and many others like it. When I am older, I will find a job that will make my dream come true." My sister laughed at my plans and wished me luck. It did seem an impossible dream then, given the fact that girls didn't have too many job opportunities those days.

But destiny would come to my help. I was studying in Hindu college when I saw an advertisement in the papers

Fighting for recognition in a male dominated society

calling for applications for the post of air-hostesses for Indian Airlines. This seemed just the thing for me.

Always filmy!

Unapologetically ambitious

I was around eighteen years of age and the financial situation at home had worsened over the years, with many of those who knew or lived with us taking loans from my 'trust-all' mother and never returning them. We did not have any meaningful regular income and were on a shoe-string budget those days. So, the advertisement, for the post of air-hostesses, was a Godsend for me and I applied immediately for the job.

Thousands of girls like me had applied for the posts. The airlines shortlisted hundred; and I was thrilled to find my name on that list. There were grilling interviews and group discussions after that, over three days. Luckily, thanks to the academic ambience at home, I was quite well-read and up-to-date with current affairs. So, I sailed through these sessions.

When my name appeared on the list of ten selected persons, my happiness knew no bounds! I had done it all on my own! Indian Airlines was just three years young when I joined it, a symbol of a fast-developing new country. When I draped the light-blue, silk georgette sari, slipped into the black sandals and carried the black hand bag that were a part of my uniform, I felt I had stepped into a whole new

Donning the IA uniform

[10]

world! Like our country, which was ten years old, I was full of aspirations and determination and unapologetically ambitious. My dreams were taking shape, high above the ground. They were literally soaring. The works hours entailed hard work, yes; but there was never a dull moment. The four-week training had been rigorous. Contrary to popular opinion, the job of an air-hostess was not just a glamorous one. You had to be empathetic to all passenger needs. Celebrities like film-stars, kings, queens, politicians as well as non-celebrities, all had to be looked after well. Those with special needs required special care and we were trained to do all this.

The crew for one of my first flights

Apart from hospitality protocol, we were taught to face various kinds of emergencies, from oxygen mask deployment to rectifying air-conditioning malfunctions. We were taught, both in theory and practice, the nitty-gritty of what it takes for an airplane to fly, with numerous passengers on board. Handling crises like cabin de-compression and unplanned landing were all part of the drill.

Here, I will take a detour to narrate an amusing incident. When I reported, on my first day for training, at the Human Resources department, at the Indian Airlines headquarters, in Connaught Place, a senior official welcomed us newcomers and asked us to introduce ourselves. When he heard my surname was a Bengali Sinha, he expressed deep shock. In a very discouraging voice he said the job was not for Bengali girls! I don't know whether he thought I would be too conservative or too shy for the job. Whatever the reason, he declared that I would not last beyond a month. This was very demoralising, but it also spurred me on to prove him wrong. Thereafter, whenever I met him, I would jokingly remind him that I had lasted well beyond his prophecy, and happily so.

Taking Flight

My first flight was a Delhi-Calcutta-Delhi one, on a Sky-Master with 44 passengers. The cabin crew consisted of me and our all-India head of air-hostesses. I was a bit nervous, especially when I had to make the in-flight announcements in English, but fortunately all went well; and my chief complimented me at the end of the flight. Over the years, I developed a very good rapport with her and she always supported me very strongly. Because of her faith in my abilities, I was often put on flights that had high-profile Indian and international passengers. This widened my world even more, far more than I had dreamt of as a young teenager, in a modest hotel in Shimla.

The Skymaster aircraft

One morning, I was on the standby roster…and I was suddenly asked to report as crew for a chartered flight. At the airport I was very pleasantly surprised to learn that the king and queen of Bikaner were on that flight. The reason for them chartering a flight was, however, a sad one. They had just lost their aunt and so had to rush home, to Bikaner.

The beautiful Gajner Palace

I learnt so much about the grace and culture of royal families on that flight. The raja and his wife were humility personified, apologising profusely to the crew for pulling them out of their homes on a holiday. When we reached Bikaner we found the entire city in mourning because the Rajmata had passed away. Nonetheless, the king organised a royal tour of the city for us, including an elaborate one of the famous Gajner Palace, built on the edge of a lake and known as the jewel of Thar Desert. Such was the etiquette of the privileged in those days.

On another occasion, I was on a flight that had Maharaja Sawai Man Singh and Maharani Gayatri Devi of Jaipur with us, and what a pleasant experience it was! My father had last worked with the Jaipur State Treasury and though he had passed away over a decade earlier, Maharaja Man Singh fondly recalled interactions with him. Warm and courteous, he asked me about my job as well, and spoke animatedly about his passion for polo, a sport he excelled in. Seeing I knew nothing about the latter, he offered to send me a book on it.

Card from Maharaja of Jaipur

It was not an empty promise. That new year I received a handsome tome on the game together with a new year's card that had him and three other Maharajas in polo attire.

[15]

For many years, thereafter, I received new-year cards with his signature and the seal of the state of Jaipur on them.

There were so many such exciting moments. In 1959, President Marshal Tito of Yugoslavia visited India with much fanfare. After his meeting with the government in Delhi he flew to Hyderabad and Madras, accompanied by Ms Tarkeshwari Sinha, among the first women politicians of India, and Captain S. M. Nanda, future admiral of the Indian Navy, in official capacity. I was privileged to be on board their national carrier on special deputation. They were a team of 17 Yugoslavian crew members and I was the only Indian representative. We struck up a fantastic

Autograph of Marshal Tito

rapport and the Yugoslavians invited me to their country after we went sight-seeing in ours. Interestingly, Ms Sinha spent a lot of time with me on this journey and she also urged me to join her team promising to keep me under her tutela ge. It was an exciting trip and I definitely felt a few inches taller after meeting such important personalities, at such close quarters!

Another time, I had the opportunity to be on duty when Indira Gandhi was on board. She was then the Minister of Information and Broadcasting. Not very communicative, she had her nose in a book throughout the flight. Even when the lights dimmed, and other passengers dozed off, she continued to be engrossed in her book.

On yet another occasion, Dr. Karan Singh, the son of the last ruling Maharaja of Jammu and Kashmir, Hari Singh, was on the same flight that I was allotted. Very polite, very cultured, he had an eloquent manner of speaking. In later years, he held the portfolio of Tourism and Civil Aviation in the Union Cabinet, the youngest member to do so.

I had the privilege to be on board with several very cultured celebrity passengers regularly, which included dignified actors like Dilip Kumar, Pran and Raj Kumar. Dilip Kumar was the only person, in all my years of flying, whose autograph I asked for. He gave it very charmingly, saying it was his pleasure. Not surprising that he had such a large fan following. Not known to me then, my future husband would be a close friend of his and I would get to meet him often after marriage.

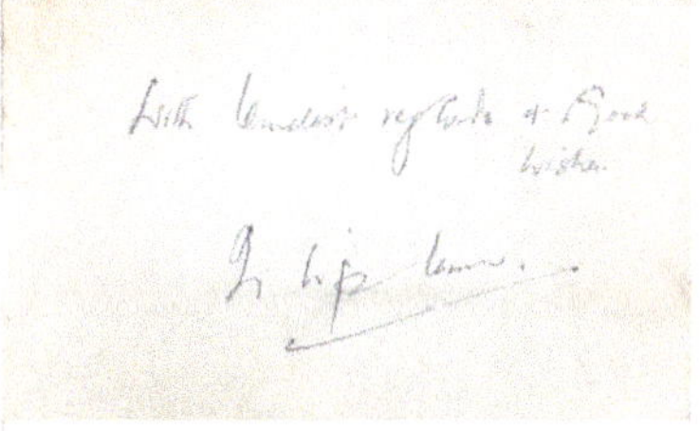

Autograph of Dilip Kumar

My husband with evergreen Dilip Kumar

As I have mentioned earlier, these were all memorable moments that were way beyond my dreams. When I had vowed to stay in hotels like the Cecil in Shimla, I never expected then that I would stay at many such hotels, some even more grand-- The Taj in Bombay, the Falaknuma in Hyderabad, the Great Eastern in Calcutta…While the

The Cecil Hotel, Shimla

grandeur of these hotels was something else altogether, visiting cities like Rangoon, Karachi, Hyderabad, Srinagar, Jaipur, Bombay gave me a glimpse into different histories

One of the sight-seeing outings between flights

and terrains. Srinagar was a romantic, pristine town with very friendly people. Hyderabad had historical structures like the Golconda Fort and Salarjung Museum.

Its people were, however, not too outgoing. We didn't see too much of Rangoon but the little that we passed by, on our way to and from the airport, was rustic and scenic. I didn't see much of Karachi, either, because the riots etc. had happened a few years before and so we didn't venture out into the city at all. Jaipur had a special place in my heart because of my father. Its people were also very warm and friendly and there was much to see historically.

But my absolute favourite was Bombay. The drive from the Taj Hotel to the airport via the splendid Marine Drive, the fascinating film studios in the suburbs...I was totally smitten by this city.

At the time, I never imagined that I would one day accompany my husband to Bombay and

Marine Drive, Mumbai

live in an apartment on Marine Drive. Taking liberties with an old Scottish proverb, I would say if wishes were horses little girls would fly!

Meeting luminaries from diverse fields, travelling across the country, dealing with different situations, my job as an air-hostess was a learning experience few girls of my age would have been exposed to, in the 1950s.

There was one experience I will never forget. It was the 27th of May, 1959... I was scheduled to fly to Karachi, as part of the crew, on a Viscount. The Viscount was a British-manufactured, 44-seating, four-engine turbo, suitable for flying medium distances.

We took off from Delhi and reached Karachi very smoothly. The return flight was at 4 pm. It so happened that PIA, the Pakistan national carrier was also flying to Delhi, around the same time. Since they served free alcohol on board, most passengers preferred to take their flight. We had only three passengers on ours. My fellow crew member and I looked forward to an easy flight, hoping to catch up with one other.

How wrong was our assumption! Midway through the flight we started facing very bad weather and the captain switched on all warning signs, with instructions to fasten our seat belts. What followed over the next 30 minutes was harrowing, and that is putting it mildly! Torrential rain and hail-stones pounded our aircraft from all sides. At a flying height of 16000 feet, the hail-stones were huge, much larger than what we see at ground level. Suddenly, there was a deafening noise from the tail end and black smog engulfed us. Thinking it was smoke, we feared the worst—that the tail had caught fire.

Luckily, that wasn't the case. But with the smog and resultant de-compression our ears got totally blocked and we could hear nothing. The hail, meanwhile, continued to relentlessly pound the windows, doors and wings. Suddenly, the plane hit an air pocket and we fell from 16000 feet to 10000! My seat belt ripped off and I fell forward but I kept holding on to the broken belt. For a split second the aircraft steadied and I rushed to another seat to fasten up again. With the sudden drop in altitude, we had bags flying out, on to us from the overhead shelves. Food trolleys with heavy flasks started rolling down the aisle. Fortunately, we had only three passengers so nobody got badly hurt. But their ashen faces said it all. For thirty minutes, which seemed like an eternity, the nightmare continued.

When things looked a bit stable I rushed to the cockpit. What I saw was horrifying! The hail had shattered the windscreen and Captain Garewal had been hit on the head. He was bleeding profusely but had managed to navigate thus far by tying his shirt around his head. His co-pilot had been recently commissioned and probably would not have known how to tackle this crisis.

How the captain saw us through till Delhi and landed safely was nothing short of a miracle. Fire engines had rushed to the tarmac to evacuate us. When we disembarked and saw the aircraft we were stupefied! The wings were very badly damaged, the window screen had broken…the plane looked like it had come out of a war zone. Luckily, the fuselage had held! Call it luck, destiny or our captain's nerve, all of us survived. We learnt later that a military aircraft flying through the same zone had crashed. Since we were not loaded with passengers, thanks to PIA's free-liquor service, our plane had pulled through.

All of us were sent on forced leave for 15 days. The aircraft was de-commissioned and later sent to UK for repairs. Government of India showed its appreciation for our captain's courage and presence of mind by awarding him a gallantry award.

While the above was an exceptional experience on the Karachi-Delhi route, flights from Delhi to Srinagar were, as a routine, tricky. We had to go through the narrow Banihal Pass, with mountains, precariously close, on both sides, in a Dakota that could not fly above the mountains.

The aircraft, those days, did not have the sophisticated navigational equipment you have today; and much depended on the pilot's skill to take us through safely. Once, as we manoeuvred our way through the pass, one of the engines started sputtering and stopped working completely just after we had got through. Somehow, the

The Banihal pass, Kashmir

pilot took us till Srinagar and managed to land. But just about. The landing gear, too, gave way, and we landed at an angle, resting on a wing. This is where all the emergency evacuation measures we had been trained for came into practical use, as I had to help ensure all the passengers got out safely from a tilted aircraft!

The Dakota aircraft

Taking care of passengers, whether they were VIPs or not was an intrinsic part of our training. Empathy for those with special requirements was another aspect of our profession. I remember, on the flight to Karachi, whose return trip was so hazardous, there was one elderly gentleman struggling with his seat belt and his food tray. His hands were quivering, and sensing that he had a medical issue, I gently asked him if he needed help. He nodded a yes, very gratefully; so I sat next to him and fed him his meal and helped him drink his coffee too. He was very touched because he didn't think he would get such attention and he thanked me profusely and even dropped a note of appreciation to my chief.

On another flight, I found myself, unwittingly, playing agony aunt to an American lady who must have been around 60 years old. For some odd reason, she felt so comfortable with me that she narrated the reason why she had come to India as a tourist. A botched love affair with a Sikh man in New York, who eloped with her best friend, had caused her so much of trauma and embarrassment, that she had set out a world tour with a group of ladies of her age to overcome her emotional distress. At the end of the flight she took my address and would regularly send me letters telling me about her life. She was quite clearly very lonely, and for some time I replied to her letters. Gradually, due to my busy schedule, we lost touch.

My life as an air-hostess, certainly, didn't lack excitement. Different flights, different passengers, different situations, there was always something new happening on every flight. Once, we had singers Mohammed Rafi and Geeta Dutt on board- such talented, famous artistes with not an iota of snobbery! When I hesitantly requested them to sing, they obliged quite happily. We piled up some blankets and cushions for them at the rear end of the plane and they regaled us with one popular number after another. They came back to their seats only when safety belts had to be strapped on, before landing. Do you think this would have been possible today? That was an era when celebrities wore their fame with humility and grace.

One of our flights was called a slow-service flight because from Delhi to Calcutta, it stopped at Lucknow, Varanasi and Patna, to cater to tourists. During a return flight from

Calcutta, we were once diverted to Gaya due to rough weather. Gaya was a small airport without any hotel facilities nearby.

Gaya airport

We had to spend the night at the airport as night flying was not permitted. So it became the cabin crew's responsibility to make 22 passengers comfortable for the night in the airport lounge. Fortunately, most of them were very sporting foreigners who looked upon this unscheduled halt as an adventure. While three crew members went out into the town to buy food for everybody, I had to take care of passenger comfort in the lounge. We managed to get some rooms, normally reserved for VIPs, to accommodate the women. After we ate Gaya cuisine, played some games, laughed and joked, and I even sang a song, the men sprawled out on the sofas and the ladies slept in the VIP rooms. The next morning all of us washed up in the bathrooms of the airport and boarded our flight to Delhi. Passenger care in the most adverse situations was a part of

[24]

our job profile, and most times we rose to the challenge rather admirably, I must say.

There were less challenging experiences too. Of the glamorous kind. One morning when I walked into my chief of cabin crew's office, she smiled at me and said one Guru Dutt had called her from Shimla to enquire about me. She was hesitant to share any information about me but once he revealed who he was and the purpose of him wanting my contact details, she decided to check with me before giving him any information. The artistic actor-director was in the throes of casting for his film Kaagaz Ke Phool and he was keen to cast me as the leading lady.

And, so it happened, that I met the filmmaker in Bombay, in the lounge of The Taj, where he narrated the story of his film to me. I was naturally flattered and excited but I knew it would not be easy convincing my family to let me enter films. Around the same time I had received offers for two Bengali films as well: Kanna, opposite Uttam Kumar, and Othol Joler Ahoban, opposite Shoumitra Chatterjee.

I had not told my family about any of these developments as I knew it would be well-nigh impossible getting permission from them to enter the celluloid world. But after meeting Dutt, I decided to spill the beans. As expected, all hell broke loose, and no amount of reasoning had any effect. In the 1950s, girls had little freedom and to act in films was considered crossing all limits!

With a heavy heart, I declined all the offers. Later, more offers came my way, both, from the film world as well as for modelling. And I turned them all down. Another offer that I did not take up was from British Airways. I was so happy working for Indian Airlines that I was not tempted at all to leave my comfort zone.

Some pictures from screen tests

However, one offer I said yes to, after being pursued ardently, was for marriage.

cRomance in the Air

It was a regular day at work. I was on a routine flight, in a Viscount, from Delhi to Calcutta, sometime in the month of October, 1959. The flight was full, with 44 passengers.

I was enjoying my new found freedom

Many years later, I came to know that the man I would marry, Romen Bhattacharya, was on this flight. He worked with Air India and was travelling to Calcutta with his boss. Apparently, it was love at first sight for Romen. His senior sensed the vibes and decided to play Cupid. As soon as he got the opportunity, he struck up a conversation with me. When he discovered I was a Bengali he told his junior, also a Bengali, "If I were you, I would not let her go."

That seemed to have spurred him into action. Unrelentingly, for several years, he left no stone unturned to impress me and my family. I was not at all ready for marriage at the time. I was enjoying my job thoroughly, and did not want to give up my new-found financial independence. The film and modelling offers, too, made me feel good even though I didn't take them up. Who wanted to trade all this for humdrum domesticity?

Besides, in order to prove naysayers wrong about my glamorous profession, I used to be wary of any attention from the male passengers, keeping all of them at an arm's length from me.

But this suitor was not one to be fobbed off!

A senior official with Air India, his work entailed a lot of travelling. As he knew a lot of senior employees in Indian Airlines, it was not difficult for him to find out which flights I was on and to book a seat on those flights; and then try to strike up a conversation with me. Sometimes, he would land up at the lobbies of the hotels where we were put up. Over time, I began to find this amusing but I still followed my principle of not talking too much with male passengers. He got the message. He knew I would never meet him beyond duty hours on flight.

So he found other means of wooing me. Using his network of 'informers' he landed up at my sister's husband's restaurant, Capri. Within a few minutes, he struck such a rapport with my brother-in-law that the latter took him home where he met my sister. My sister realised he was the passenger I had spoken to her about who was often, not so coincidentally, on my flights. She sized him up and decided he was 'a very fine gentleman'.

My husband, on the right, bonding with my sisiter and brother in law.

Now that he had impressed my sister and her husband with his fine manners it was not difficult for him to meet my mother, while I was away on work. Over several such visits, he won over my mother as well. My mother took up his cause and advised me to accept his proposal. Then, his mother wrote to my mother a formal letter but I was not ready to get married. Reluctantly, my mother conveyed this

Married!

message to his mother. But they continued to keep in touch, and, finally, made me give in. In December, 1962, we got married, in Delhi and Calcutta.

It was a match made in the skies, if not in heaven. Aviation history was an intrinsic part of my husband's career as well so we had much in common. Of course, his experience was far more varied than mine, as he had started his professional life with cargo airlines pan-India, with Nagpur as the hub, when he was instrumental in improving airfreight logistics. Nagpur airport served as a centre for the postal department's night mail service and my husband had often been on these mail delivery flights. Those were early days of our airlines and my husband had seen it all.

He later moved to passenger airlines. He had the privilege to fly a few times with J.R.D. Tata, with whom he had a wonderful rapport. J. R.D, as he was fondly known, founded Tata Airlines in 1932, which became Air India in 1946; and my husband always spoke very highly of J.R.D's involvement with his airlines. It seems he was so particular about customer service that, on one occasion, he, himself, started serving the meals! He was an outstanding example of humility, and his staff imbibed this from him. Tata trusted his team totally, and always expected them to make that extra effort to do better. My husband also often spoke of his very high standards of integrity. Having learnt the ropes from the father of Indian aviation, my husband, I can proudly say, was much respected in the industry and was instrumental in pioneering several initiatives in the aviation sector.

One of my husband's initiative

I quit my job after our marriage and moved to Calcutta where my husband was posted. He was with Lufthansa then. Two months later, he was transferred to Bombay. In 1963, I joined Air India's Bombay office, in the ticketing department, as I was getting thoroughly bored sitting at home. It was a new role for me and, unlike today, where everything is computerized in those days you had to look up thick ABC books to create a travel itinerary and work out the cost. It was quite complicated and in case you went wrong any short collections were debited from your personal account. It was a very tough job which required immense concentration for reasons outlined above but, on the lighter side, dramatically improved my geography as well.

A few months later my husband re-joined Air India. This created a bit of a complication as my boss was junior to my husband. This led to minor frictions at home and, eventually, I resigned in 1964.

Motherhood

There was a long sabbatical from work after that. In June 1969 I gave birth to my son, a sweet, 7.5 pound baby. My initial reaction was of panic when the doctor told me it was a boy as, all along, I had wished for a daughter. My impression of boys was not too good as I had seen mostly boisterous, stubborn sons of relatives. But the moment I held my little one in my arms I felt an amazing calm, seeing his serene face.

Over the years, I realised he was very different from the boys I had seen in my family. Far from being boisterous, he was a very caring, affectionate son, without any effort on my part. Bringing him up was such a pleasure that I didn't miss a professional life. Time went by most enjoyably. Whether it was helping him with his studies, or taking him for sports practice and other extra-curricular activities, I enjoyed every moment of being a mother.

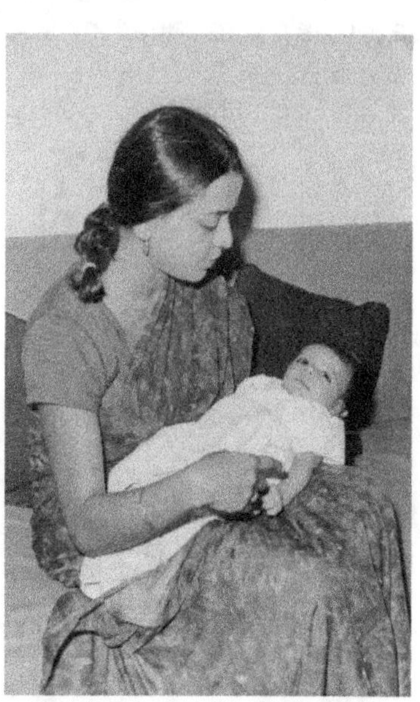

Pleasures of motherhood

When my son was around 3 years old my husband got an offer from Travel Corporation of India to set up a branch in Poona. It was 1972 and we were planning our move to

The two men in my life

Pune. While I was enjoying every moment of motherhood I was also somehow, subconsciously missing a professional life. From childhood I was always one to take new initiatives and learn new things and this time I happened to see a write-up about coding classes in Fortran and Cobol. This made me very curious and after reading up some more I was enthused enough to consider picking up a course in Coding. Fortran appealed to me since it was being used for projects such as the design of bridges and airplane structures, for factory automation control, storm drainage design, analysis of scientific data and it seemed there would be good career opportunities for me.

I had a short discussion with my sister who was visiting me at that time and she immediately encouraged me to take it up. She had always been my cheerleader! So I took up the course and though I joined a bit late I put in long hours and a lot of effort and cleared the course with quite impressive marks. Now, in some respects, you could call me a visionary because I was probably among the early adopters or learners of coding and definitely the first in the family. When we moved to Poona I thought I would be able to take up a part-time job, if not full-time, so I went and interviewed with a few organizations. Unfortunately, and as one can imagine, in those days computer and coding was not very commonly used so the only institutions that were looking to hire were the army and the meteorological department. Women were few in this space and when I interviewed at the meteorological department I could immediately sense some sort of cynicism probably even disbelief that I as a woman had taken up coding. The interviewer himself was very discouraging and as expected I wasn't made an offer. That somehow put an end to my intentions of taking up a job as a coder but I do wonder seeing the success of the IT industry over the last few decades what I could have been had I managed to get a job with an IT company in those days.

When my son entered his teens, I realised he was quite independent. So then I resumed my professional life once again. In 1982 I joined Pan American Airlines as a business representative for their Poona market. My job entailed promoting the airlines with travel agents. Since the travel industry was my calling, I revived my existing contacts and created new ones to make Pan Am's presence felt in Poona, in a big way. It was a very satisfying period, professionally, with large numbers of Indians flying to Hong Kong, Singapore and the US.

But then, striking a work-family life balance once again, I quit Pan Am in 1985, when my son was in class X, as I felt he needed all my support while studying for his board exam. This was also the year when my husband and I started our own travel agency, Leonard Travels. We were blessed to be able to put up a plush office on M.G. Road, a prime location in Poona.

My visiting card!

Both, my husband's and my earlier experience in the travel industry came in very handy. We ran the business from 1985 to 1999, with a fair share of ups and downs, like in any business. We worked well as a team. While I marketed our company and handled ticketing and clients, my husband looked after the financial side and liaised with airline companies and hotels.

Getting started with our own travel company

[35]

My son, who is quite entrepreneurial by nature, also pitched in, for four years. Together, we built a fantastic rapport with schools who trusted us with organising tours for their students, within India and overseas. My husband would work out the plans in great detail and execute them so proficiently that at one time we had around 20 prominent schools entrusting their annual educational and holiday tours to us.

My son continued his studies simultaneously, and fared well in his exams. After doing his Master in Business Administration, he joined a multi-national bank in Bombay. For a while, I missed his presence tremendously, but our business helped to divert my mind. Like all mothers, I was happy to see my son doing well in his career.

Eventually, we sold our business in 2000, and then lived in Poona, now known as Pune. While we felt sorry to let the business go since we had built such goodwill and reputation with our clients we knew it was the right thing to do since it was time for us to enjoy a retired life.

In 1999, my son married a lovely girl who became like the

Enjoying retirement years

daughter I had wanted way back in 1969. It was a peaceful, happy phase in our lives. In 2002, our happiness multiplied with the birth of our first grandson. With the birth of our second grandson in 2006 our joys doubled. By now, we had re-located to what was once Bombay, now Mumbai. Playing grandmother to two lively boys was a novel experience!

In 2010, life took an unfortunate turn with my husband developing complicated health issues after a fall. It was downhill, thereafter; and it pained all of us tremendously to see an active man like him getting bed-ridden. My daughter-in-law was my pillar of support during this time. Despite our best efforts, in 2012 my husband passed away. I miss him very much as he was a very supportive life partner, small fights notwithstanding.

Looking back on my eventful life, I have no complaints. It has been a rich, fulfilling one. I was not the kind of person to lead the lives of many girls of my generation who were forced to settle down to playing only one role, that of wife and home-maker.

The satisfaction of being all that and much more makes me a very contented person today…

www.ingramcontent.com/pod-product-compliance
Lightning Source LLC
LaVergne TN
LVHW020844200726
843508LV00003B/1062